More Team Building 20: A Team Building Card Game, By Tyler Hayden

Copyright © Tyler Hayden, 2017

Published by Tyler Hayden,
P.O. Box 1112
Lunenburg, Nova Scotia
Canada
B0J 2C0

Cover: Tyler Hayden
Illustrations: Steven Lacey
Distributed Electronically by Kindle Direct Publishing

National Library of Canada Cataloguing in Publication

Hayden, Tyler, 1974–
    More Team Building 20: A Team Building Card Game / Tyler Hayden.

ISBN   978-1-897050-50-7

Business. 2. Education. 3. Games. I. Title.

Discover More Fun @ <u>www.teambuildingactivities.com</u>

More Team Building 20: A Team Building Card Game,
By Tyler Hayden

Warning - Use at Your Own Risk

FIND THIS FOR **FREE** ... WANT TO GIVE US A HIGH FIVE TO SAY THANK YOU?
We'd love you to BUY US A COFFEE or four - we like coffee.
www.teambuildingactivities.com/store/p46/donate

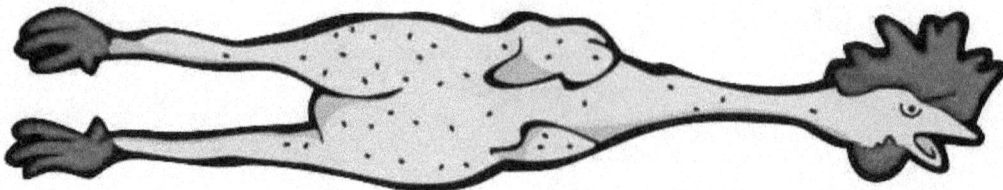

20 Series Games, By Tyler Hayden

This game takes about 10 to 25 minutes to play. It is an incredible content specific icebreaker/break-time activity that is totally inclusive. The educational intention is to encourage people to know a little more about each other in a fun and interactive way while learning a specific core content area (i.e. Customer Service, Leadership, etc). Check out our full line of Team 20 card decks at www.teambuildingactivities.com.

Remember, the priorities are to have fun and play safe.

How to play:

1. Make sure that you have a safe space for the participants to share. Schedule this activity at a time when they will be willing and open to talk to one another. I often run this event during a coffee break or to get the "cob webs" out part way through a meeting and focus the learners thoughts about our specific area of learning upcoming in our program. It is also great to pull it out when you are convening with a group you know fairly well, just for fun.

2. Place the game cards in the middle of the table along with a dice (if you don't have a dice download & make one at www.teammover.com/free).

3. The player with the longest commute goes first and rolls the dice. The person to the rollers right will pick up the card and ask the roller the question. If the player rolls a (1) a Who question is asked - (2) What; (3) When; (4) Where; (5) If; and (6) Why.

4. Once the question is read the roller answers the question. The answering is always "challenge by choice" meaning if they are uncomfortable with the question they answer. If not a new question can be drawn or they can pass on their turn.

5. Players around the table are permitted to ask follow-up questions to the person posing the answer as long as they relate to the original question asked.

6. Play continues sequentially in a clock wise direction.

7. There are two ways to "organize the play" – *Speed Version:* collectively the group answers the twenty questions total - keep track with a tally. *Longer Version:* each person answers a question from each category - keep track with a grid. Either way you need someone at the table keeping track of the "score".

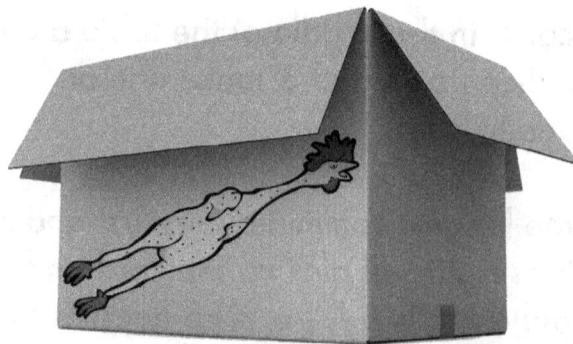

8. Have fun.

WHO 1	**makes the sexiest undergarments?**
WHAT 2	**was your favorite childhood toy?**
WHEN 3	**have you really partied?**
WHERE 4	**have you lost the most money in the shortest time?**
HOW 5	**does history predict the future?**
WHY 6	**do marriages work/not work?**

© Tyler Hayden

WHO 1	would you like to have dinner with: Einstein or Gandhi?
WHAT 2	excites you?
WHEN 3	have you felt really supported at work?
WHERE 4	were you when you wished you didn't have to leave?
HOW 5	do you define "wealth"?
WHY 6	do people feel the need to one up each other?

© Tyler Hayden

WHO 1	would catch a mouse first: Sylvester or Garfield?
WHAT 2	is more important: health or wealth?
WHEN 3	were you really brave?
WHERE 4	do you volunteer your time?
HOW 5	would you spend an extra hour every day?
WHY 6	are you a good person?

© Tyler Hayden

WHO 1	do you like to spend time with?
WHAT 2	are you famous for amongst your friends?
WHEN 3	have you demonstrated leadership?
WHERE 4	is your favorite place to go on a date?
HOW 5	do you become an invaluable resource at work?
WHY 6	do teenagers think that they are invincible?

WHO 1	would you like to be on a deserted island with?
WHAT 2	do you wish for?
WHEN 3	have you done something out of character?
WHERE 4	have you felt you were part of a community?
HOW 5	have you made a difference at work?
WHY 6	do some people need pets in their lives?

© Tyler Hayden

WHO **1**	would you like to be on a deserted island with?
WHAT **2**	do you wish for?
WHEN **3**	have you done something out of character?
WHERE **4**	have you felt you were part of a community?
HOW **5**	have you made a difference at work?
WHY **6**	do some people need pets in their lives?

© Tyler Hayden

WHO **1**	is tougher: Spiderman or Superman?
WHAT **2**	is a successful day at work for you?
WHEN **3**	were you in real trouble?
WHERE **4**	should the government spend less money?
HOW **5**	do you dream of spending your retirement?
WHY **6**	do we have unrest globally?

© Tyler Hayden

WHO **1**	makes the best junk food?
WHAT **2**	is your best childhood memory?
WHEN **3**	have you met someone famous?
WHERE **4**	were you when you were the most embarrassed?
HOW **5**	would you spend the day as our country's leader?
WHY **6**	are you a success at work and home?

© Tyler Hayden

WHO **1**	is your favorite author?
WHAT **2**	makes a great weekend?
WHEN **3**	did you realize you were an adult?
WHERE **4**	is the best place to shop: big box or boutique store?
HOW **5**	would you blow $2000 in a shopping spree?
WHY **6**	does democracy not work/work?

© Tyler Hayden

WHO **1**	**is your best friend?**
WHAT **2**	**is your greatest attribute?**
WHEN **3**	**have you lived on next to no money?**
WHERE **4**	**is your best friend?**
HOW **5**	**would you improve your office?**
WHY **6**	**do people cheat?**

© Tyler Hayden

WHO 1	was your favorite superhero or heroine growing up?
WHAT 2	makes your adrenaline pump?
WHEN 3	did you lose something special?
WHERE 4	is the greatest environmental atrocity happening?
HOW 5	are pets important to a person's life?
WHY 6	is life so precious?

© Tyler Hayden

WHO 1	has the worst job in the world?
WHAT 2	is "happiness" to you?
WHEN 3	have you really challenged yourself?
WHERE 4	would you invest $10,000?
HOW 5	do you raise great kids?
WHY 6	do people quit diets?

© Tyler Hayden

WHO 1	is your favorite musician?
WHAT 2	are you missing in your life right now?
WHEN 3	was your first kiss?
WHERE 4	is the best place to make money?
HOW 5	would you spend a night partying with your favorite rock star?
WHY 6	is it important to work hard?

© Tyler Hayden

WHO 1	has made the greatest impact on your life so far?
WHAT 2	is your biggest vice?
WHEN 3	is your favorite holiday?
WHERE 4	are your 4 top destinations to visit in the world?
HOW 5	would you change your life?
WHY 6	do people get antsy in traffic?

© Tyler Hayden

WHO 1	is a great role model for kids?
WHAT 2	is your best work memory?
WHEN 3	have you fallen in love?
WHERE 4	did you learn your biggest life lesson?
HOW 5	do you allocate the money you donate to charity?
WHY 6	is it important to act ethically?

© Tyler Hayden

WHO **1**	**was your favorite teacher?**
WHAT **2**	**do you look for in a job?**
WHEN **3**	**were you the most thankful?**
WHERE **4**	**would you like to blow $10,000?**
HOW **5**	**do you spend your time on weekends?**
WHY **6**	**is the Internet so important?** © Tyler Hayden

WHO **1**	has the best job in the world?
WHAT **2**	is your greatest job skill?
WHEN **3**	did you make the greatest deal?
WHERE **4**	do you like to hang out with friends?
HOW **5**	would you describe a "perfect vacation"?
WHY **6**	was Oprah such an influence on society?

© Tyler Hayden

WHO 1	would win a cage match: Donald Trump or Martha Stewart?
WHAT 2	can you do and lose all track of time while you are doing it?
WHEN 3	were you a hero/heroine?
WHERE 4	is the most unique place you have visited?
HOW 5	is it mother in laws get such a bum rap?
WHY 6	does Disney do "that" to kids?

© Tyler Hayden

WHO **1**	was your first crush?
WHAT **2**	do you like about your car?
WHEN **3**	did you learn to drive?
WHERE **4**	should every child visit?
HOW **5**	were your parents right, but you hate to admit it?
WHY **6**	should we challenge ourselves?

© Tyler Hayden

WHO 1	is the happiest person you know?
WHAT 2	is the funniest thing that has ever happened to you?
WHEN 3	will you retire?
WHERE 4	do you like to go to celebrate an achievement?
HOW 5	would you spend the day as James Bond?
WHY 6	do we put stock in what other people think of us?

© Tyler Hayden

WHO **1**	**is the greatest businessperson of all time?**
WHAT **2**	**are you afraid of?**
WHEN **3**	**have you started over?**
WHERE **4**	**can you buy the best desserts in town?**
HOW **5**	**do you feel about paying taxes?**
WHY **6**	**is it important to find satisfaction at work?**

© Tyler Hayden

WHO **1**	**is the most loving/caring person you know?**
WHAT **2**	**is your favorite hobby?**
WHEN **3**	**were you the most proud of yourself?**
WHERE **4**	**is a place everyone should visit?**
HOW **5**	**is life different for kids today, then when you were young?**
WHY **6**	**do people fall in love?**

WHO **1**	is the sexiest person alive?
WHAT **2**	is the best travel destination?
WHEN **3**	are you frustrated?
WHERE **4**	is your most prized possession?
HOW **5**	adventuresome are you?
WHY **6**	is coffee so addictive?

© Tyler Hayden

WHO 1	is the craziest person you know?
WHAT 2	is your favorite possession?
WHEN 3	have you made the greatest change in your life?
WHERE 4	can you buy the best bargains?
HOW 5	do you get engaged at work?
WHY 6	is our society hooked on fast food?

WHO 1	was the worst leader of a country?
WHAT 2	are you empowered by?
WHEN 3	are you happiest?
WHERE 4	would you get a tattoo, and of what?
HOW 5	has someone helped you out of a bad predicament?
WHY 6	do people design weapons of mass destruction?

© Tyler Hayden

A Message for you.

Dear Team Mover,

We are so thankful you chose to share one of our 20 Series Books with your Team. We are passionate about helping connect people in meaningful ways by brining the world books, activities and tools like this - because we think people matter.

As we move forward in publishing this (and other) series of books and games, we need your help to build a community of people with that same authentic desire to create meaningful relationships with the people they work with. We ask you join us and share our work with your friends, colleagues and families.

Here are some of the ways that we can stay connected and you can find more resources (link to the appropriate social media links on the sites):

Team Building - www.teambuildingactivities.com
Keynotes & Consulting - www.tylerhayden.com
Books & Consulting - www.14minutementor.com
Books & Giving - www.messageinabottlebook.com

Look forward to connecting soon. Best of continued success my fellow team mover - the work you are doing matters.

Tyler

www.ingramcontent.com/pod-product-compliance
Lightning Source LLC
Chambersburg PA
CBHW051235200326

41519CB00025B/7389